The Wise Owl Guide to...
Dantes Subject Standardized Test (DSST)

Principles of Public Speaking
Second Edition

Copyright © 2009 Wise Owl Publications, LLC

All rights reserved. No part of this book shall be reproduced, stored in a retrieval system, or transmitted by any means, electronic, mechanical, photocopying, recording, or otherwise, without written permission from the publisher. No patent liability is assumed with respect to the use of the information contained herein. Although every precaution has been taken in the preparation of this book, the publisher and author assume no responsibility for errors or omissions.

Printed in the United States of America

ISBN-10: 1449590497
ISBN-13: 9781449590499
Library of Congress Control Number: 2009912022

Cover design © Wise Owl Publications, LLC

© 2009 All Rights Reserved.
DSST is a registered trademark of Prometric.
This book is not affiliated with Prometric.

Table of Contents

- Introduction 5
- About the Test 6

Part I. Ethical, historical and social considerations 7
- Seven elements of a speech 7
- Free speech in a democracy 8
- Free speech issues 8

Part II. Audience analysis 9
- How to analyze an audience and why 9
  - Types of analysis 10
  - Preparing a speech to the needs of the speaker and characteristics of the audience 11

Part III. Topics and purposes of speakers 13
- Speech topics 13
  - Selecting a topic 13
- Speech purposes 15
  - Speeches and conversations 16

Part IV. Structure and organization of public speech 17
- Structuring introductions 17
- Structuring bodies 17
- Structuring conclusions 18
- Understanding thought patterns 19
- Organizational strategies 19

Part V. Content and supporting materials 20
- Recognizing and using evidence 20
  - Materials of support 20
  - Credibility 21
- Argument and reasoning 22
  - Fallacies 22
- Formulating appeals 23
  - Emotional appeals 23
  - Logical appeals 24
- Visual aids 25

Part VI. Research 26
- Reference materials 26
  - Citation of evidence 26
  - Tips for sucessful research 26
- Finding sources 27

- PART VII. LANGUAGE AND STYLE 30
  - LANGUAGE APPROPRIATE FOR PUBLIC SPEECH 30
    - MEANINGS OF WORDS 30
    - RHYTHM 31
- PART VIII. DELIVERY 32
  - ARTICULATION 32
  - VOICE 32
  - PRONUNCIATION 33
  - BODY ACTION 33
  - METHODS OF DELIVERY 33
- PART IX. COMMUNICATION APPREHENSION 34
  - UNDERSTANDING AND CONTROLLING APPREHENSION 34
- PART X. LISTENING AND FEEDBACK 35
  - LISTENING TECHNIQUES 35
    - TYPES OF LISTENING 36
  - OBSTACLES TO AVOID 36
  - GIVING AND RESPONDING TO FEEDBACK 36
- PART XI. CRITICISM AND EVALUATION 37
  - CRITICIZING 37
  - EVALUATING THE EFFECTIVENESS 38
- PART XII. PREPARING FOR THE SPEECH 39
  - STRUCTURE ORGANIZATION 39
    - PREPARATION 40
    - CREATING YOUR SPEECH 41
  - DELIVERY 43
  - CONTENT/SUPPORTING MATERIAL 43
  - EFFECT/PERSUASIVE 43
  - LANGUAGE/STYLE 44
- LIST OF APPENDICES 45
  - APPENDIX A: PERCENTAGES OF EXAMINATION PART I 46
  - APPENDIX B: PERCENTAGES OF EXAMINATION PART II 48
  - APPENDIX C: CLUSTER EXAMPLE 49
  - APPENDIX D: COMMONLY MISPRONOUNCED WORDS . 50
  - APPENDIX E: PRACTICE SPEECH SUBJECTS 51
- GLOSSARY 52
- PRACTICE TEST 68
- ANSWER KEY 88
- INDEX 95

INTRODUCTION

Are you going to learn everything about public speaking in this study guide? Absolutely not! But… are you going to learn enough to pass the DSST test? Yes! In this book we focus on what you need to know, that is it. The DSST (Dantes Subject Standardized Test) series tests cover what is most commonly taught in a college course. That leaves out a lot of content that might be taught in a formal class. Prepare for this test with this study guide and you will be well on your way to a degree in significantly less time than hitting the books in night school (this is not to say it is any easier to get a degree this way, just more flexible)! This book is written in a format that's easy-to-read, understand, and remember. Public speaking is a fascinating real-world topic, and no matter if you have a test to pass or not this information will make you feel like a more educated person for knowing it. Even if you *think* you know everything there is to know about public speaking, this book will teach you a thing or two!

About the Test

This test is divided into two parts. The first part is a multiple-choice test consisting of 84 questions.

The exam (and this book) covers topics such as:
- Ethical, historical and social considerations
- Audience analysis
- Topics and purposes of speeches
- Structure and organization
- Content and supporting materials
- Research
- Language and style
- Delivery
- Communication Apprehension
- Listening and feedback
- Criticism and evaluation

This test book includes an 84-question practice test to ensure a solid handle on the course information.

The second part of this test requires the student to record a persuasive speech that is approximately four minutes in length. The speech topic will be given to the test-taker with 10 minutes to prepare for delivery. The speech will be recorded for grading. This book covers how to prepare for the speech and sample speech topics.

PART I. ETHICAL, HISTORICAL AND SOCIAL CONSIDERATIONS

This test is divided among many areas of public speaking. This portion of the test will account for approximately five percent of the questions. Part I will cover:

- Free speech in a democracy
- Free speech issues

SEVEN ELEMENTS OF A SPEECH

There are seven key elements to a speech:

- **Speaker**
    - The person presenting the material/oration.
- **Message**
    - The communication being conveyed.
- **Channel**
    - How the message is being conveyed (speech, telephone, etc).
- **Listener**
    - The person(s) receiving the message.
- **Feedback**
    - The message delivered back to the speaker.
    - Feedback is typically nonverbal.
- **Interference**
    - Any obstacle in understanding the message.
    - Interference can be internal or external.
- **Situation**
    - Time and place of a speech

ETHICAL CONSIDERATIONS

Ethics is a branch of philosophy that examines right and wrong. Ethics are important in public speech. Speakers need to adhere to several guidelines when preparing to speak including:

- Ethical goals
    - Ensure that the goals are in line with your beliefs and values.

- Proper preparation for a speech
    - Research well so incorrect information is not passed through the speech.
- Be honest
    - Do not lie about statistics, quote out of context, pass along insufficient findings, and provide false proof.
- Do not be mean
    - Even if name-calling can be protected under the Free Speech clause in the First Amendment it is not ethically responsible.
- Avoid plagiarism
    - There are several types of plagiarism they are:
        - **Global** – an entire speech or idea is one other person's or groups.
        - **Patchwork** – ideas and languages from multiple places are taken.
        - **Incremental** – failure to give credit for parts of an idea or speech.
- **Quotations** – if exact words are used from someone else's speech, credit the original speaker.
- **Paraphrase** - when using someone else's ideas in your own words you still need to give authorship credit.

FREE SPEECH IN A DEMOCRACY

The first Amendment of the United States Constitution protects the right to free speech, religion, and expression.

FREE SPEECH ISSUES

However, there are types of speech that are NOT protected under free speech. They are:

- Fighting words
- Defamatory speech
- Reckless disregard for the truth

PART II. AUDIENCE ANALYSIS

This portion of the test will account for approximately eight percent of the questions. Part II will cover:

- How to analyze an audience and why
- Preparing a speech to the needs of the speaker and characteristics of the audience

HOW TO ANALYZE AN AUDIENCE AND WHY

The demographics of an audience should be taken into consideration. The demographics include:

- Age
    - Age is an important aspect of a person's outlook.
    - Age will affect what someone knows about (historically and references) and can affect what they believe is appropriate.
- Sexual orientation
- Ethnicity
- Socioeconomic status
    - Income
    - Occupation
    - Education
- Religion
- Political affiliation
- Gender

Careful consideration should be made to not over-generalize an audience based on their demographics (**stereotyping**).

After the demographic analysis, the **situational audience analysis** should be examined. These include:

- Size of the audience
    - The larger the audience the more formal the presentation.
- Physical setting of the speech
    - Be aware of any physical limitations of the room (too hot, cold, crowded).
- Disposition of the audience toward the topic
    - Interest

- Be aware of the interest the audience has for the topic before your speech.
  - Knowledge
    - Determine how much the audience knows about your topic.
  - Attitude
    - Know how the audience feels about the topic.
- Speaker
  - The more highly respected the speaker is in their field, the more receptive the audience.
- Occasion
  - Understand the meaning of the gathering.

TYPES OF ANALYSIS

Analyzing an audience takes observation and conversation. There are also tools that can be used to assess the audience, including:

- Interviewing
  - Face to face, and very effective; but inefficient in time and cost.
- Questionnaires
  - Three major types of questions:
    - Questions that offer a choice between two or more answers (**fixed alternative**).
      - Have you read the play "Hamlet" by William Shakespeare?
        - Yes____ No ___ Can't remember ___
    - Questions that ask for an answer on a scale of answers (**scale questions**).
      - On a scale of 1-5 (1 meaning dislike and 5 meaning enjoyed) did you enjoy the Hamlet play?
    - Questions that ask for any answer (**open-ended questions**).
      - Who was your favorite character in the play, and why?

PREPARING A SPEECH TO THE NEEDS OF THE SPEAKER AND CHARACTERISTICS OF THE AUDIENCE

During the presentation and preparation of a speech the speaker should always keep the audience in mind (**audience centeredness**). To become audience centered ask these questions:
- Who is the speech directed to?
- What is my specific purpose?
- How can I effectively convey my purpose?
    - Try to determine responses and have answers for them either addressed in the speech or ready to give when asked.

The speaker should try to create a bond with the audience (**identification**). Identification can be accomplished by focusing on common:
- Values
- Goals
- Beliefs
- Experiences

Next, examine the **situational audience analysis** (time, place, and setting of the speech). Based on the information you can determine your speech should be appropriate, timely, and foster interest:
- Is the size of the audience very large? Then a more formal speech is called for.
- Try to resolve any physical limitations of the setting, if the physical limitations cannot be helped try to make the speech as entertaining as possible to refocus the audience on the message and not their discomfort.
- Try to discern the audience's interest, knowledge, and attitudes on a topic.
    - Generate interest with the introduction.
    - Don't give the audience more information than they can digest (especially if there is limited knowledge on the topic).
    - Try to know in advanced the attitudes on the topic so the speech can incorporate addressing concerns, and answering issues.
- Make your best impression to try to alleviate any negative judgments on the speaker.
    - If the speaker is a recognized expert in the field include this information in the introduction.

- Be cognizant of why people are together.
    - Do not veer off of the main purpose of the gathering (i.e. turning an informative speech into a sales pitch).
    - If people's expectations aren't met on the occasion the message will likely be rejected.

Sometimes, no matter how much preparation is done with the audience in mind the speaker will find that they've lost the audience during the speech. Be aware of this and recapture your audience while speaking. If this is a speech that will be reused, be sure to tailor your speech for the next time based on this feedback.

- Example: The time is shorter than you were told initially
    - Solution: Don't talk faster; highlight the main points instead.
- Example: You see quizzical looks in the audience.
    - Solution: Clarify the point for the audience, or back up and explain a little better.

PART III. TOPICS AND PURPOSES OF SPEAKERS

This portion of the test will account for approximately eleven percent of the questions. Part III will cover:

- Speech topics
- Speech purposes

SPEECH TOPICS

Speech topics to be chosen are typically:

- Topics that the speaker knows a lot about.
    - Speeches that are based on the experience of the speaker.
    - The speaker will know more about this topic typically than their audience.
- Topics that the speaker wants to know more about.
    - Topics chosen because the speaker wants to learn as well as the audience.
    - Sometimes these speeches can be something the speaker cares deeply about.

SELECTING A TOPIC

People can find it very difficult to select a topic on which to speak. However, in the "real world" typically a speech is dictated by an occasion or event.

People that have trouble finding the subject of a speech can:

- Brainstorm for topics
    - Personal inventory
        - Jot down hobbies, experiences, interests, and skills.
        - Review the listing and try to find a subject among the list (even by grouping some together). For example:
            - Volunteer work and gardening
            - Both can be combined to discuss growing food for the homeless shelters.
    - Clustering
        - If the personal inventory is not successful clustering can be used.

- A paper is divided into nine columns and list the first five or six items that come to mind under each (an example of a cluster can be found in Appendix C):
  - People
  - Places
  - Things
  - Events
  - Processes
  - Concepts
  - Natural phenomena
  - Problems
  - Plans and policies
- Many will likely come out as potential topics.
- Take the few that are most interesting and jot them down.
- Free-associate ideas and you may come up an original concept.
  - Other places to find topics
    - Reference search
    - Encyclopedias and other reference material
    - Internet search

SPEECH PURPOSES

Public speaking is when a speaker delivers a message with a specific purpose to an audience of people. The goal of communication is to have a shared meaning by the end of the speech. The **general purpose** of a speech is the broad goal of the message. There are several general purposes of speeches:

- **Inform** –used with a purpose of comprehension.
    - Objects
        - Informing about a person or thing.
    - Processes
        - Informing about a series of actions and the result.
    - Events
        - Informing about something that has happened.
    - Concepts
        - Informing about an idea or belief.
- **Persuade** – used when trying to have an impact on a belief or audience action.
    - Fact
        - Used to persuade audience to accept the view of the facts.
    - Value
        - Used to persuade audience to accept the value (rightness or wrongness of an action).
    - Policy
        - Used to persuade the audience on a specific course of action.
    - Passive agreement
        - Encourages audience to believe that an action is a good one without actually inciting the audience to do anything.
    - Gain immediate action
        - Encourages audience to take steps in order to support the policy/idea.
    - Tips for persuasive speaking
        - Enlist the listener in a cause by changing attitudes or inciting action.
        - Attempt to influence audience choices.
        - Try to limit the alternatives.

- Seek a response.
- **Entertain** – a speech with the sole purpose of entertainment.

Once the general purpose has been identified, the **specific purpose** is exactly what the speaker hopes to accomplish. Before planning the speech, the speaker should know exactly what they want the listener to take away from it.

Example of the topic, general purpose, and specific purpose:

Topic	General Purpose	Specific Purpose
Charity	Persuade	Garden vegetables to give to charity.

Finally, there is the **central idea** of the speech. The central idea will summarize the main points that the speech will address.
- Central idea example:
  - Gardening is a simple, cost effective method that can be done to benefit the poor.
  - Most speeches have between two and five main points.

SPEECHES AND CONVERSATIONS

Speeches are not the same as conversations, but they have many similarities including:
- Logical organization of thoughts.
- Tailoring a message to the listener.
- Telling a story for the most impact.
- Adapting to feedback.

There are three distinct differences between a public speech and a conversation:
- Speeches are more structured.
- Speeches are more formal.
- Speeches are delivered differently.

PART IV. STRUCTURE AND ORGANIZATION OF PUBLIC SPEECH

This portion of the test will account for approximately eighteen percent of the questions. Part IV will cover:

- Structuring introductions
- Structuring bodies
- Structuring conclusions
- Understanding thought patterns
- Organizational strategies

STRUCTURING INTRODUCTIONS

An introduction's purpose is to gain the attention and interest of the audience. A successful introduction will accomplish many things:

- Get the speaker off on the right foot.
- Arouse the audience's interest.
- Preview the speaker's topic.
- Create a good first-impression/bond to the audience.
- Boost the speaker's confidence.
- Establish speaker credibility.

Methods used for a successful introduction include:

- Providing a quote.
- Asking a question.
- Using humor.
- Telling a story.
- Presenting a visual aid.
- Arousing curiosity.

STRUCTURING BODIES

Work on the body of the speech first because the body will help dictate the introduction and the conclusion. Primary attention is given to the substance of a speech, which is largely found in the body. There are several steps to save time and energy in the structuring of the speech:

- Start with an outline
  - The outline will ensure that you are addressing your central idea and achieving the specific purpose.
  - The main points (which are addressed in your central idea) should be conveyed in a single sentence.
    - Most speeches have between two and five main points.
  - Do not include more than one idea in each point (look out for the words "and" or multiple verbs).
  - Support each main idea
    - If you find that you have too many points to support one idea you may need to break it up into two main ideas.
    - If there are too few supporting points, then the main idea may actually be a supporting point for another main idea.
    - If the main point has too few supporting ideas additional research is necessary.
  - Transition from points with grace.

STRUCTURING CONCLUSIONS

A conclusion's purpose is to end the speech and reinforce the main points. A successful conclusion will:

- End strongly.
  - Quotation
  - Dramatic statement
  - Reference to introduction
- Revisit main points.
- Leave an impression on the audience and challenge them to respond.

Two types of endings for a speech are:
- Dissolve ending
  - Generate emotion appeal and fade to a dramatic final statement.
  - A farewell statement often is a dissolve ending.
- Crescendo ending
  - Speech builds to more intensity.

Understanding thought patterns

Much of the interpretation of a speech is happening beneath the surface (the audience is not sharing all of their thoughts). The speaker should attempt to hold a mental conversation with the audience.

Organizational strategies

Organize the speech in what would make the most logical sense for impact. Some of the most common organizations are:

- **Chronological**
    - Presents main point in the time continuum order they occur in.
- **Spatial**
    - Describes lay out, structure, and direction.
- **Causal**
    - Organized by cause and effect order.
- **Problem solution**
    - Explains a problem and identifies a solution.
- **Topical**
    - Presents evidence in no specific order.

Part V. Content and Supporting Materials

This portion of the test will account for approximately fifteen percent of the questions. Part V will cover:

- Recognizing and using evidence
- Argument and reasoning
- Formulating appeals

Recognizing and using evidence

Evidence is used for many purposes including:

- Illustrating a point in the speech.
- Elaborating an idea.
- Proving the truthfulness in a statement.

Not every piece of written or spoken word is considered evidence to support an argument. Before using evidence in a speech the speaker should consider several factors:

- Background of author
- Credibility of publication
- Reliability of data
- Date of publication

Materials of support

Materials used to support a speaker are:

- Examples are used to clarify, reinforce, and personalize the idea. There are three types of examples:
    - Brief
        - Specific case to discuss one point.
    - Extended
        - A lengthy story to illustrate a point.
    - Hypothetical
        - A fictional example.
- Statistics are used to quantify, and should be simplified and used sparingly.
    - Presentation of numerical data via graph or other visual aid.
- Testimony is used to support a point.
    - Expert
        - Given by experts in a field

- o Peer
    - Given by someone with firsthand knowledge

CREDIBILITY

One of the most important tools in the speaker's arsenal is credibility. Credibility is made up of:
- Competence
    - o How the audience regards the speaker's expertise.
- Character
    - o How the audience regards the speaker's trustworthiness.

There are three types of credibility:
- Initial
    - o The credibility perceived before the speaker starts his/her speech.
- Derived
    - o The credibility perceived during the speech.
- Terminal
    - o The credibility perceived at the conclusion of the speech.

Some ways to boost credibility are:
- Explain why you should be seen as an expert on the topic.
- Create a bond with the audience.
- Orate with conviction.

Argument and reasoning

Reasoning is the formulation of a conclusion based on evidence presented. There are four different types of reasoning:
- Reason from specifics
    - When reason begins with specific facts and moves to a general conclusion.
- Reason from principle
    - When reason begins with a general principle to a specific conclusion.
    - Example:
        - Fact: All plants need water.
        - Fact: The marigold is a plant.
        - Conclusion: The marigold needs water.
- Casual reason
    - Reason to form a cause and effect relationship.
    - **False cause** in this reasoning is common. False cause assumes that since one event precedes another the first event automatically caused the second.
- Analogical reason
    - Comparing two similar events and assuming what is true for one will be true for the other.
    - Example:
        - If you are good at track and field you'll be great at soccer.
    - An **invalid analogy** is when the two things being compared are not really alike. For example, soccer is a competitive team sport while track and field is an individual one.

Fallacies

Reasoning can be subject to errors (**fallacies**). There are five main fallacies with reasoning:
- **Red herring**
    - Introduction of an irrelevant fact to divert attention.
- **Ad hominem**
    - Attack on the person not the issue (common in politics).
- **Either – or**
    - Assuming there are only two solutions when there are more.

- **Bandwagon**
  - The idea that if something is popular, then it is correct.
- **Slippery slope**
  - Beginning a process will inevitably lead to subsequent steps.

Formulating appeals

The two main appeals are emotional and logical. There are different tactics in both appeals. However, a good persuasive speech will have a healthy blend of both.

Emotional appeals

Emotional appeals are intended to make the audience feel. The emotional appeal is the most powerful. Some of the feelings a speech can elicit are; fear, admiration, guilt, empathy, and anger. Emotional appeals have the capacity to inspire people and can be quite powerful (Adolf Hitler used emotion, but so did Martin Luther King, Jr.). Therefore, appealing to emotions should be done responsibly.

Persuasive speeches often use emotional appeals. Some methods of generating emotional appeals are:

- Emotional language
- Imagery
- Sincerity

There are six general emotions that all cultures/ages express. They are:

- **Fear**
  - Unpleasant feeling of pending danger.
- **Anger**
  - Feeling ranging from irritation to rage.
- **Surprise**
  - Feeling of amazement at something unexpected.
- **Sadness**
  - Morose feeling of unhappiness.
- **Disgust**
  - Feeling of repulsion and distaste.
- **Happiness**
  - Feeling of contentment.

Additionally, there are three secondary emotions that are expressed differently based on age/gender/culture:
- **Pride**
    - Feeling of respect for a person, thing, or accomplishment.
- **Guilt**
    - Feeling of wrongdoing.
- **Shame**
    - Feeling of embarrassment.

LOGICAL APPEALS

Logical appeals are an attempt to persuade the audience by reasoning. The two main types of reasoning are inductive and deductive:
- **Inductive**
    - Starts with a specific case and moves to a general conclusion.
        - Example:
            - All observed plants need light to grow.
            - Therefore, all plants need light to grow.
    - Best to use when audience believes differently than the speaker.
- **Deductive**
    - Starts with a general conclusion and moves to a specific one.
        - Example:
            - The president wants to spend too much money.
            - He wants to bail out the banks and Wall Street.
    - Best used with the audience is more likely to support the speaker.

VISUAL AIDS

Visual aids can add interest, but should be chosen only if they can aid in the understanding of the message.

- Why use visual aids?
    - Adds interest.
    - Aids in comprehension.
- General tips on visual aids
    - Prepare them in advance.
    - Keep them simple.
    - Readable for the entire audience.
- Types of visual aids
    - Charts
        - Visually depicts numbers and statistics.
    - Objects
        - Large enough for the audience to see.
        - Don't pass it around it will become a distraction.
    - Maps
        - To help determine geographic relationships to each other.
    - Models
        - Used when the object cannot be brought in.
    - Drawings
        - Make sure all labels can be read.
    - Photographs
    - Slides and transparencies
    - Computer graphics
        - Can be integrated into other medias to give them a more "polished" look.
    - Multimedia presentation
        - Be careful that it isn't too much.
        - Do enough to aid in understanding.

PART VI. RESEARCH

This portion of the test will account for approximately five percent of the questions. Part VI will cover:

- Reference materials
- Finding sources

REFERENCE MATERIALS

When using evidence to support a claim ensure that the name, qualifications, and time of evidence are given. To determine the validity of claims made on resources you should evaluate the information closely (especially internet).

Ask yourself these questions:
- Is the author clearly identified?
- Is the author an expert on the topic?
- Who is sponsoring the information? A business, an individual, the government? Is it someone with a bias on the information? A reputable expert?
- How new is the document? Is the information no longer valid because of the age?
- Is the evidence specific enough?
- Is the evidence novel enough?

CITATION OF EVIDENCE

When using evidence information must be collected to cite the source of the information. The citation information includes:
- Name of author
- Title
- Volume or edition number, if applicable
- Name, date, and place of publishing information
- Page where the information can be found

TIPS FOR SUCESSFUL RESEARCH

There are several things that can be done to set up for success in the researching of a speech.
- Start early
    - Just like studying for this test – don't procrastinate!

- Make a bibliography
    - Jot down where you think you will get the information you need.
    - You may not use all of the sources when the research goes deeper.
    - Take good notes and effectively record where the information comes from.

FINDING SOURCES

There are several places where sources can be found:
- Libraries
    - Librarians
    - Catalogue
        - Usually found via computer at the library.
        - Can typically search by:
            - Author
            - Key word
            - Publisher
            - Title
        - A **call number** identifies the location of the book at the library.
    - Periodical database
        - Identifies articles from a large database of periodicals.
    - General database
        - Houses several non-book pieces of literature.
    - Special database
        - Houses specialized information about a subject.
- Newspapers
- Reference works
    - Encyclopedias
        - **General** – provides basic information about all knowledge.
        - **Special** – devotes to one specific piece or type of knowledge.
    - Yearbooks
        - Almanacs
        - Facts of File
    - Dictionaries

- Quotation books
- Biographies
- Atlases
- Gazetteer
- Internet
  - Search engines
    - Google
    - Yahoo
    - Alta Vista
  - Metasearch engines (submits the request to many search engines)
    - Dogpile
    - Metacrawler
  - Virtual libraries
  - Specialized resources
    - Government sources
    - References sources

Finding sources already documented are not the only answer. Investigative interviews can be done to acquire the information necessary for a speech. There are several steps to a successful interview:

- Prior to the interview
  - Identify what you hope to accomplish.
  - Decide who would be able to answer the questions.
  - Arrange the logistics (the who, what, when, where, and why).
  - Determine if the interview will be recorded (and ask permission to record the person being interviewed).
  - Prepare the questions.
    - Do ask questions that are:
      - Reasonable
      - Direct
      - Specific
    - Don't ask questions that are:
      - Things you can answer without the interview.
      - Leading
      - Hostile
- At the interview
  - Dress appropriately, and be on time.
  - Repeat the purpose of the interview.

- Set up recording equipment (if they have agreed).
- Don't stray from the topic.
- Listen to the speaker attentively.
- Don't stay too long (end it when you said it would end).
- After the interview
  - Review and transcribe your notes.

Part VII. Language and Style

This portion of the test will account for approximately eleven percent of the questions. Part VII will cover:

- Language appropriate for public speech

Language Appropriate for Public Speech

Choose words carefully when speaking.

- Use words that are familiar.
- Try to use concrete words.
- Use as little words as necessary to convey the message (stop the clutter).
- Use imagery
  - Simile
  - Metaphor
- Use words that are inclusive (does not demean any group).
- When discussing a group use the words they use when referring to themselves.

There are some styles of speech that you should avoid, they are:

- Clichés
  - Overused expressions such as; look before you leap.
- Jargon
  - Words related to a specific profession.
- Ethnocentrism
  - The belief that one culture or group is better than another.
- Stereotypes
- Hate speech
- Avoid using "he" to refer to men and women

Meanings of Words

Words have two types of meanings **connotative** (the feeling that someone gets from a word) and **denotative** (the actual meaning). Note the difference in the below sentences:

- We are here today to find each orphan a house.
- We are here today to find each orphan a home.

Both sentences say exactly the same thing, however a feeling of home brings warmth and family, while house is just a structure. Be aware of the connotation of words and use them wisely.

RHYTHM

Rhythm is important to a speech because it is created by the choice of words. There are several ways a speaker can improve the rhythm of a speech including:

- **Parallelism**
    - Similarity in arrangement between points or phrases.
- **Repetition**
    - Repeating a word or phrase for emphasis.
- **Alliteration**
    - Repetition of the same initial sounds (usually consonants) in order.
- **Antithesis**
    - Juxtaposition of contrasting ideas.

PART VIII. DELIVERY

This portion of the test will account for approximately eleven percent of the questions. Part VIII will cover:

- Articulation
- Voice
- Pronunciation
- Body action

ARTICULATION

Articulation is the crispness of the distinct speech sounds. Ensure that you are taking the time to articulate the sounds of the words (no mumbling or slurring). The following are some examples of common articulation issues (outlined in bold).

- **Howya' doin'**?
- I **dunno** I think I **otta** go.
- You **wanna'** come?
- Ok, I **hafta** go now, see **ya'**.

VOICE

The seven factors of voice control are:

- Volume
    - Controls the impact of a message.
    - Determined by room size, number of people, microphone use, and background noise.
- Pause
    - Used to signal the ending of a thought.
    - Controls speaker's impact on an audience.
- Pitch
    - The high or low of a person's voice.
    - Used to emphasize points.
- Pronunciation
    - The phonetics of the spoken word.
- Articulation
    - The crispness of the distinct speech sounds.
- Dialect
    - The accent that identifies a person's ethnicity.
- Rate
    - The speed of the speaker's words.

Pronunciation

Pronunciation is the phonetics of the spoken word. Make sure you know how to pronounce all words in the speech. Look up technical words and the pronunciation and practice saying them correctly. See Appendix D for frequently mispronounced words and how they "should" be said.

Body action

Body language can enhance or undermine the message of the speaker. The types of body language are:

- Movement
    - Natural movement necessary to the speech.
    - Avoid nervous movement.
- Gestures
    - Your gestures should be natural.
- Eye contact
- Personal appearance
    - Always "dress the part".

The purpose of body action and other nonverbal cues in a speech are to:

- Clarify the message.
- Establish a relationship with the audience.
- Establish credibility for the speaker.

Methods of delivery

There are four methods of delivery:

- **Manuscript**
    - Reading the speech verbatim.
    - Used most commonly when words will be recorded.
- **Memorization**
    - Reciting a speech that has been remembered.
- **Impromptu**
    - A short speech with little or no time to prepare.
- **Extemporaneous**
    - A carefully planned and prepared speech.
    - Uses a brief outline that the speaker refers to.

PART IX. COMMUNICATION APPREHENSION

This portion of the test will account for approximately three percent of the questions. Part IX will cover:

- Understanding and controlling apprehension

UNDERSTANDING AND CONTROLLING APPREHENSION

Even people that communicate without any anxiety throughout life may freeze up when in front of people. Nervousness before making a speech is normal and actually can assist in making a better speech by helping the speaker prepare more thoroughly. The nervousness causes a surge of adrenaline in the speaker. Research suggests that women may experience higher rates of anxiety then men when speaking publicly.

Factors that cause speaking apprehension are:

- Lack of experience speaking in front of people.
- Having a different point of view from the audience.
- Awkwardness about being the center of attention.

Some methods of controlling apprehension are:
- Speak publicly whenever possible (practice makes perfect).
- Extensively prepare
    - Each minute of speaking time takes approximately 1-2 hours of preparation time.
- Think positive.
- Visualize the speech as a success.
- Realize that people probably will not know you are nervous.
- Don't expect to be perfect.

Some other ideas that can be used to help with apprehension are:
- A good night's sleep.
- Tighten and relax muscles before going onstage (provides an outlet for the adrenaline).
- Slow breaths.
- Make eye contact with the audience.
- Concentrate on communication.
- Use visual aids to avert the attention from yourself.

PART X. LISTENING AND FEEDBACK

This portion of the test will account for approximately five percent of the questions. Part X will cover:

- Listening techniques
- Obstacles to avoid
- Giving and responding to feedback

LISTENING TECHNIQUES

It is important to note that hearing and listening are NOT synonymous. Hearing is natural, while listening is actually paying attention to what is said.

Seven ways to improve listening are:

- Take it seriously.
- Actively engage:
    - Give attention to the speaker.
    - Make an effort to understand the message.
- Tone down the distractions.
- Avoid distractions of appearance and delivery.
- Don't judge before the message is relayed.
- Focus on listening:
    - Try to discern main points.
    - Listen for support to the main points.
    - Learn to effectively deliver your own speeches based on other speakers' weaknesses and strengths.
- Take strong notes:
    - **Key-word outline** – outline that briefly touches on the main points of the speech.

Three ways to improve **ethical listening** are:
- Be nice and pay attention.
    - The speaker has put significant time and effort into the speech.
- Avoid prejudging the speaker.
    - Do not judge someone based on appearance.
- Be open-minded.

TYPES OF LISTENING

There are four types of listening:

- **Appreciative**
    - Listening for pleasure
- **Empathetic**
    - Listening as a counselor
- **Comprehensive**
    - Listening to understand
- **Critical**
    - Listening to determine validity

OBSTACLES TO AVOID

Seven methods of poor listening are:

- Lack of concentration.
    - When the brain gets bored it can start wandering to other things.
    - The brain can process 400-800 words per minute, while we can speak about 120-150 words per minute.
- Listening too intently.
    - Trying to remember every thing that is said can make the meaning and facts get lost.
- Jumping to conclusions.
- Focusing on the wrong things.
    - Too much time spent making judgments about dialect, dress, or presentation.

GIVING AND RESPONDING TO FEEDBACK

Feedback is the listener's response to a message.

- To facilitate feedback:
    - Prepare answers to possible questions.
    - Positively answer questions.
    - Address answers to the entire audience.
    - Listen carefully to the question.
    - Don't digress from the topic.

PART XI. CRITICISM AND EVALUATION

This portion of the test will account for approximately eight percent of the questions. Part XI will cover:

- Criticizing
- Evaluating the effectiveness

CRITICIZING

Proper criticism on public speaking is difficult to find. Friends are often too kind, and others are often too harsh. For a self-study course such as this one, you may find it best to record yourself and study your own weaknesses to shore them up. While watching and listening to other speeches be cognizant of where the speech is effective and where it is not. This will help develop your own speech style.

It is difficult for anyone to endure criticism. Here are some helpful hints on criticism:

- Everyone has critics. Not one person is universally liked. With the billions of people in the world, you too are bound to have critics. The more public you are, and the more public speaking you do, the more critics you'll have. If you don't want critics, then don't speak. Ever.

- When being criticized try to look past the emotion and understand the other person's point of view. This takes a great amount of maturity (some of our government leaders still struggle with this). Who knows, maybe you'll change your mind? Embrace criticism as an opportunity to learn and grow.

- No person can MAKE you feel anything. You make yourself feel however you want to feel. Don't let someone else's criticism effect how you feel about yourself. Take what you need from criticism and move on.

- Just because you listen to someone's criticism doesn't mean you have to agree with it. Not everyone has to agree all of the time. If you examine their point and don't find merit, then move on. Don't dwell on needless negativity.

- Understand and deal with the fact that some people will not agree with you.

EVALUATING THE EFFECTIVENESS

To evaluate the effectiveness of a speech you need to examine the following:

- Did the speaker get the demographics of the target audience right?
- Did the speaker convey their moral character (**ethos**)?
- Was sound reasoning used for a persuasive speech (**logos**)?
    - Strong evidence
    - Valid support to claims
- Was the speech organized in an easy-to-follow format?
- Was the language appropriate, purposeful, and effective?

PART XII. PREPARING FOR THE SPEECH

The second part requires the student to record a **persuasive speech** (used to influence an audience's beliefs, values, or acts) that is approximately four minutes in length. The topic will be given to the student with ten minutes of preparation time. There are several reasons for automatic failure on the speaking portion including:

- Timing (shorter than three or longer than five minutes)
    - Don't be alarmed about this! Be sure you are cognizant of the time as you are speaking and when you have one minute left make sure you have hit your main point and bring that point home with the conclusion.
- Topic not addressed
    - The topic is given to you, make sure you use it and don't free-associate to something else entirely.
- Failure to take a position
    - This is NOT a speech to inform. Realize that. You must have an opinion and justify why you are right.
- Taking several positions
    - You will need to persuade somebody either way of something. You will FAIL if you take a position and then discuss the merits of the other side of the position. Take one side and stick to it.
- Editing

After reading this section practice, practice, practice! Use Appendix E in this book for the speech preparation subjects. Put together outlines, deliver, and time yourself. If possible record yourself so you can find places that need improvement before the big day. Remember there is only a ten-minute preparation period.

STRUCTURE ORGANIZATION

This portion of your speech attributes to 25 percent of your final score. Ten to fifteen percent of the speech should be made up of the introduction and the conclusion. No matter the length, every speech has three parts:

- Introduction
    - Should be used to make people interested and want to hear more.
    - Should make the audience understand what the speech is about.
- Body
    - Strong transitions should be used between points so the audience knows when the next point is being talked about.
- Conclusion
    - The conclusion should summarize the speech and for a persuasive speech encourage the audience to think, act, or believe the point of view of the speaker.

PREPARATION

You are only given ten minutes to prepare so quickly move through the following steps for your speech (the graders KNOW you only have ten minutes and no one is expecting perfection).

- Preparation outline
    - This will outline the main points and is discussed more below under "creating your speech".
    - Be sure to take a stand on the issue and defend why you did.
    - Try to persuade the audience to side with you.
    - Don't spend more than 3 minutes on this.
- Read your preparation outline
    - Check for how long it will run, quickly go through the points, and spend 3 minutes on this step.
- Hone your outline
    - Make sure it has only the key points and rehearse the speech (quickly). When you have to speak you will slow it down but ten minutes is not enough time for a full dress rehearsal of your speech.

- o You should have rehearsed so much before the test that this should come easy to you.
- Make final adjustments and deliver.

CREATING YOUR SPEECH

For the test you already know what kind of speech you have to give (**persuasive**). Be sure to work fast on this because you have ten minutes to prepare for your speech (which can go very quickly because this is the first time you've seen the topic). Be sure to practice with the ten-minute speech preparation from this book so you can have more confidence in what you can accomplish in that limited time.

Let's say we were given the topic: Uniforms in public school

- Now we know two factors
    - o The topic (uniforms in public school).
    - o The general purpose (persuasive).
- Next we need to take a stand in one direction or another (**specific purpose**). Use a complete sentence and thought. This is exactly what you want the audience to "take away" from your speech. Make sure it meets the assignment.
    - o The specific topic may be "to persuade the audience that government steps should be taken to institute uniforms worn in public schools to establish equality among students."
        - ▪ Your specific purpose shouldn't have figurative language. (Ex. Uniforms should be used because then everyone is "cool").
        - ▪ Your purpose should be limited. Don't include too much. Use the topic the test gives you and stick to it.
        - ▪ Don't make the purpose to general (although that shouldn't be a problem if you stick to one side of an issue given to you on the test).
        - ▪ Make sure that your purpose isn't too big for the time allotted.

- Don't tackle the whole issue, just what you can to meet your purpose.
    - There are a lot of reasons that uniforms can be or not be worn. Don't go into everything. You won't have time.
- Don't make the point to trivial.
    - For example: Uniforms should be worn and the colors should be black and white.
    - Black and white have nothing to do with the topic that was asked and you'll likely fail.
- Don't make the point technical
    - Avoid jargon and the nitty gritty of the topic.
    - Be sure to get your stance out there and justify it.
- Then, determine the "central idea" of your topic. The central idea is a statement that captures the main ideas of your speech.
    - In our example the central ideal may be: "Uniforms allow children to shift their focus from economic differences to personal merit and education".
    - From the central idea we can determine that two main points have to develop:
        - Children that don't wear uniforms experience ridicule in school based on economic differences.
        - Children that wear uniforms are more likely to focus on personality and learning.

DELIVERY

This portion of your speech attributes to 25 percent of your final score. When preparing your notes outline the key terms and phrases you want to discuss. Do NOT try to record your speech on paper word for word. You will run out of time!

The test will give you the subject, ask for a stance, and provide a brief demographic of the audience. Make sure that you are keeping in mind the audience the test has given you. Also watch your volume, pitch, pauses, articulation, and pronunciation. The best method to ensure you are adequately delivering is to record yourself when practicing. Review your recordings and make corrections. This may be a bit uncomfortable, but practice makes perfect and you'll be a pro at test-time!

CONTENT/SUPPORTING MATERIAL

This portion of your speech attributes to 20 percent of your final score. Obviously you will not be able to research and provide evidence that supports your point of view. However, you DO need to make points to support your cause, and properly justify your stance.

EFFECT/PERSUASIVE

This portion of your speech attributes to 20 percent of your final score.

Persuasive speeches accomplish three goals:

- Influence choices
- Limit alternatives
- Seek a response

Make sure that you are trying to PERSUADE someone to think or do something. This is not an informative speech. For the uniform example the central idea is to encourage people to seek government steps to institute uniforms in school To ensure this objective is met the conclusion of this speech may include a sentence similar to this:

> Example: Uniforms will help children to learn and play more effectively. To help make this a reality each one of us can contact our local government representative via their

website. We can take steps together to make public school uniforms a reality.

LANGUAGE/STYLE

This portion of your speech attributes to 10 percent of your final score. Language and style refer to the following:

- Clearness
    - Good volume.
    - Appropriate vocabularies (avoid jargon and choose simple over complex).
- Use language that is interesting:
    - Metaphors and similes
    - Analogies
    - Solid descriptions

LIST OF APPENDICES

Appendix	Description
Appendix A	Approximate Percentages Examination Part I
Appendix B	Approximate Percentages Examination Part II
Appendix C	Cluster Example
Appendix D	Commonly Mispronounced Words
Appendix E	Practice Speech Subjects

Appendix A: Percentages of Examination Part I

Percentage	Curriculum Content
5%	**Ethical, historical and social considerations** • Free speech in a democracy • Free speech issues
8%	**Audience analysis** • How to analyze and audience and why • Preparing a speech to the needs of the speaker and characteristics of the audience
11%	**Topics and purposes of speakers** • Speech topics • Speech purposes
18%	**Structure and organization of public speech** • Structuring introductions • Structuring bodies • Structuring conclusions • Understanding thought patterns • Organizational strategies
15%	**Content and supporting materials** • Recognizing and using evidence • Argument and reasoning • Formulating appeals
5%	**Research** • Reference materials • Finding sources

Percentage	Curriculum Content
11%	**Language and style** • Language appropriate for public speech
11%	**Delivery** • Articulation • Voice • Pronunciation • Body action
3%	**Communication apprehension** • Understanding and controlling apprehension
5%	**Listening and feedback** • Listening techniques • Obstacles to avoid • Giving and responding to feedback
8%	**Criticism and evaluation** • Evaluating the effectiveness of a speech

APPENDIX B: PERCENTAGES OF EXAMINATION PART II

Percentage	Curriculum Content
25%	Structure/organization
25%	Delivery
20%	Content/supporting material
20%	Effect/Persuasive
10%	Language/Style

Appendix C: Cluster Example

People	Place	Thing	Event	Process	Concept	Natural	Problem	Plan and Policy
Grand-parents	U.S.	I-phone	Birth	Writing	Solar power	Tornado	National debt	No Child Left Behind Act
Obama	NYC	Desk	Funeral	Garden	Going "Green"	Flood	Real Estate	Face recognition
Pupil	Cave	Book	Wedding	Reading	Homesteading	Tsunami	Homeless	Megan's Law
Biden	Campsite	Coffee	Thanksgiving	Voting	Telecommuting	Forest Fires	Outsourcing	Bill of Rights
Clinton	Egypt	Barbie	Grad.	Cooking	Recycling	Thunderstorm	Teen pregnancy	Patriot Act

APPENDIX D: COMMONLY MISPRONOUNCED WORDS

Word	How they are commonly said	How they SHOULD be said
miniature	MIN-i-ter	MIN-ee-a-cher
genuine	GEN-you-wine	GEN-you-win
utmost	UP-most	UT-most
err	AIR	UR
escape	EX-cape	ES-cape
arctic	AR-tic	ARC-tic
federal	FED-rul	FED-e-rul
barbed wire	BOB-wire	BARB-ed-wire
et cetra	EX-set-ra	EC-set-ra
library	LIBE-air-ee	LIBE-rare-ee
often	OFF-en	OFT-en

Appendix E: Practice speech subjects

Here is an example of subjects that are frequently discussed in college level speech classes. Be familiar with these and practice speaking on these subjects. The more practice with the preparation and delivery of a speech the more comfortable you'll be during the test.

- Should the government require uniforms in public school?
- Should drug testing be allowed in the workplace?
- Should the government have stricter gun control?
- Should graduating high school students be required to give government/military service?
- Should college athletes receive pay?
- Should colleges consider race when accepting applicants?
- Should the drinking age be lowered to 18?
- Should abortion be illegal?
- Should the government be responsible for public health care?
- Should social security be privatized?
- Should the death penalty be banned?

Audience examples

Practice the above speeches with different audiences. Some example audiences are:
- A co-ed college auditorium
- A retirement home
- A political convention
- A room of teachers
- A group of political leaders
- A room of high school seniors
- A men's sports team
- Members of the military

Glossary

Because this is a study guide, some of these words are found throughout the text, however there are some new ones, be sure you understand the meanings to all of these words because they will help you exponentially during the multiple choice test. Remember what you can, make flashcards for the rest, and quiz yourself a lot, you won't regret it!

Abstract – summary of a magazine or article not written by the author

Abstract words – words that discuss ideas and concepts

Acceptance speech - speech that gives thanks for public recognition

Active listening – making genuine effort to understand the speaker's point

Ad hominem – a fallacy that attacks the person not the issue

Adrenaline – a hormone that responds to physical or mental stress

Agenda – the items to be accomplished during a meeting

Alliteration – repetition of the same sounds (normally in the initial consonants of two or more words)

Analogical reasoning – comparing two cases and assuming that the outcome for the first will be the outcome for the second

Analogy – extended story/metaphor/simile that compares something familiar to something unfamiliar to aid in understanding

Anecdote – brief real-life story

Animation – transition in the PowerPoint slide

Antithesis – use of the juxtaposition to state the point

Appreciative listening – listening for pleasure

Articulation – physical sound of speech

Atlas – book of maps

Attitude – predisposition of response that is either positive or negative

Audience analysis – gathering information about listeners that will assist in tailoring the message to them to elicit a response that is desired

Audience centeredness – keeping the audience in mind during preparation and delivery of a speech

Bandwagon – assumption that something is right because it is popular

Bar graph – compares two or more items in a visual aid

Beliefs – the way a person interprets reality (includes religion)

Bibliography – list of sources

Bill of Rights – first ten amendments to the United States Constitution

Biographical aid – reference that provides information about people

Bookmark – a feature that can store a "favorite" website for the user

Brainstorming – problem solving with the generation of many ideas

Brief example – a small illustration of a specific point

Burden of proof – obligation of the persuasive speaker to inspire change

Call number – number assigned to a library book to determine location

Catalogue – listing of all books a library has

Causal reasoning – idea that the preceding action causes the subsequent ones

Central idea – a summary of the main ideas of a speech

Central processing – where listener devotes full attention to critically thinking of the message

Channel – how a message is delivered

Chart – usually as a list summarizing a lot of information

Chronological pattern of arrangement – the points are relative to each other (the order is important)

Cliché – an expression that is overused

Close-ended questions – small range of specific answers supplied by the person asking the question

Clutter – more words than necessary

Commemorative speech – speech paying tribute to someone or something

Comparative advantages order – organizing persuasive speeches so that each main point explains why speaker's solution is better than a different solution

Connective – word or phrase that connects ideas

Circle pattern of arrangement – arranging one idea that leads to another and finally the last idea leads back to the speech thesis

Comprehensive listening – listening to understand (a student to a teacher)

Co-culture – social community whose values/beliefs are dissimilar

Concept – belief, theory, or idea

Concrete words – words that refer to items that are tangible

Connective – words that indicate relationship between phrases

Connotative meaning – the feeling a word elicits (e.g. a house is a structure and a home is some place a family lives)

Consensus – group decision that is binding

Contrast – statement of differences

Conversational quality – presenting a speech that sounds spontaneous (even if it is not)

Counterproductive roles – roles that are negative in achieving a goal

Credibility – perception of qualifications of speaker

Crescendo ending – building the points and intensity and ending the conclusion strong

Criteria – standards that judgments are based on

Critical listening – listening to determine fact from opinion

Critical thinking – organized thinking to establish the difference between fact an opinion

Delivery cues – speaking outline that gives hints on next part of speech

Demographics – statistical characteristics of a population/audience

Denotative meaning – the basic definition of a word, regardless of how the word makes people feel (e.g. house and home are the same)

Derived credibility – credibility based on the delivery of the speech

Descriptive statistics – statistical numbers that help describe things

Designated leader – person appointed leader of a group

Dialect – accent, grammar, or vocabulary differences that indicate an ethnic background

Direct quotation – testimony given verbatim

Dissolve ending – taking the intensity down and ending the speech poignantly

Dyadic Communication – conversation between two people

Egocentrism – concerning self more with own values and beliefs

Eight by eight rule – when making a presentation not more than eight words on a line and eight lines on a slide

Either/or – fallacy that there are only two solutions

Emergent leader – someone who emerges as a leader in a group

Empathetic listening – listening to emotionally support

Enthymeme – presentation of a probability

Ethical decisions – decisions between right and wrong

Ethnocentrism - assuming superior stance of religion or ethnicity

Ethos – appealing to the moral character

Etymology – word's history

Evidence – supporting materials to prove a point

Example – specific cased used to illustrate a point

Expectancy outcome values theory – the conscious evaluation of costs and benefits to an action

Expert testimony – findings by someone that is recognized in the field (e.g. psychologist testifying on someone's psychological condition)

Extemporaneous speech – extensively prepared speech that is orated based on brief notes

Extended example – a long illustration to discuss a specific point

Eye contact – visual contact with audience

Fair use – copyright law that allows students and teachers to use some copyrighted material for education

Fallacy – reasoning error

False cause – the incorrect belief that one event caused another just because it preceded it

Feedback – message delivered back to the speaker from the listener

Fixed-alternative questions – questions with limited answers available

Frame of reference – sum of a persons beliefs, values, goals, and experiences (no two people are alike)

Gazetteer – geographical dictionary

General encyclopedia – contains a little information about all human knowledge

General purpose – broad goal of speech (persuade, inform)

Generic 'he' – using a male pronoun to discuss both men and women

Gestures – Speakers' hand and arm movement during speech

Global plagiarism – taking someone else's idea and passing the entire idea off as your own

Goodwill – audience perception of the speaker's motivation

Graph – visual depiction of statistics

Groupthink – accepting ideas without critical analysis

Halo effect – the natural inclination to assume someone is good or bad in one category based on another.

Hearing – sounds entering the ear

Hypothetical example – a fictional situation to illustrate a point

Identification – when the speaker seeks to create a bond with the audience over shared values, beliefs, experiences, or attitudes

Imagery – vivid language to help give the audience a mental picture

Implied leader – group member who becomes leader based on seniority, etc

Impromptu speech – speech delivered with little to no preparation

Inclusive language – language that does not stereotype or patronize any group

Incremental plagiarism – failing to give credit for someone else's idea

Inferential statistics – statistical presentation of facts that are used to predict things

Inflections – changes in pitch and tone

Informative speech – intended to increase audience's awareness of a situation/topic

Initial credibility – credibility of speaker before they orate

Inoculation – the degree that the audience has arguments ready to answer when their beliefs, values or attitudes are challenged in a speech

Interference – anything that provides an obstacle from the listener receiving the message

Internal preview – gives the audience a glimpse of what will be discussed next

Internal summary – highlights speech points before moving on to another part of the speech

Invalid analogy – a fallacy; comparing two things that are not really alike

Invisible web – databases and resources that are not indexed by search engines

Issue based conflict – audience tests and debates ideas and solutions

Jargon - specialized language to a profession

Key-word outline – outline that briefly touches on the main points of the speaker

Kinesics – study of body language

Lay testimony – an account given by a non-expert

Leadership – ability to influence people

Leading question – question that leads someone to answer to agree with the speaker's bias

Line graph – used to show changes in numbers over time

Listener – person receiving a message

Listening – paying close attention to what is heard

Loaded question – question asked to reinforce the agenda

Logos – persuasive appeals on an audience's logic

Main point – major ideas discussed in speech

Major premise – general case

Manuscript speech – a speech written word for word

Matching hypothesis – the idea that people with be-friend other people with similar levels of attractiveness

Mean – average of numbers

Median – middle of a group of numbers

Mental dialogue with audience – mental conversation between audience and speaker during a persuasive speech

Message – information being delivered to a listener by a speaker

Metaphor – comparing two things without the use of "like or as"

Metasearch engine – groups many search engines together to give several matches to a request

Minor premise – specific case

Mode – most frequent number in a group of numbers

Model – a built to scale object of something larger

Monotone – speaking without a change in inflection

Monroe's motivated sequence - organization of persuasive speech to seek action. The five steps: Attention, need, satisfaction, visualization, and action.

Multimedia presentation – speech combining several types of video, visual aids, and audio

Name calling – derogatory words used to defame a person or group

Narrative pattern of arrangement – short story

Negation – defining something by explaining what it is not

Nonverbal communication – communication based on body language, expressions, and gestures

Open-ended questions – questions that allow the respondent to elaborate as much as they want

Operational definition – describing the meaning of something by what it does

Organizational chart – a pictorial of the group's hierarchy

Panel discussion – formal conversation on a given topic

Pathos – appealing to emotions

Paralanguage – how something is said (not what is said)

Parallelism – similar arrangement of words throughout the speech

Paraphrase – stating a recorded idea in your own words

Patchwork plagiarism – taking ideas from various sources and passing them off as your own

Pause – a brief break in a speech, usually to emphasize a point

Peer testimony – testimony from a non-expert based on first-hand experience

Periodical database – research aid that houses magazines and journals

Peripheral processing – lacking motivation to give subject the full attention

Personal based conflict – audiences argues with each other instead of focusing on topics

Persuasive speaking – intended to influence an audience's attitudes, beliefs, values and acts

Pie graph – shows percentages visually

Plagiarism – claiming someone else's work as your own

Positive nervousness – controlling nervousness to help make a speech better

Presentational meeting - information delivered during business environment

Preliminary bibliography – list compiled early of possible sources of information for research

Preview statement – a statement in the introduction that identifies the point of the speech

Primary research – research conducted first hand through interviews, surveys, etc

Problem/solution pattern of arrangement – describing a problem and justifying the solution

Pronunciation – proper sound of a word

Question of fact – truth or fallacy of a statement

Question of policy – determination of a specific course of action is necessary

Question of value – determination of whether something is right or wrong

Quoting out of context – using a statement to distort the meaning given by the person

Rate – speed of person's speech

Reasoning – drawing a conclusion based on evidence

Recency – the idea of what a person hears last has the greatest effect

Red herring – introducing an unrelated issue to divert attention

Reference work – a book that puts all information in an easy-to-find format

Repetition – using the same words or sets of words in a speech

Research interview – interview used to gather information for a speech

Residual message – the lasting message that the speaker wants the audience to remember after they leave

Rhetorical question – question that is answered mentally

Rhythm – pattern of sound the speech makes

Scale questions – designed to measure the level of agreement or disagreement with issues

Scanning – shifting gaze throughout the room to the listeners

Search aid – program used to find information on Internet

Search engine – indexes web pages to match request

Signpost – language-indicating where the speaker is in their speech ("in conclusion")

Self-fulfilling prophecy – also known as the Pygmalion Effect: if a person thinks of themselves as funny, clever, or stupid they will act in accordance with their thoughts

Simile – comparing two things using "like or as" e.g. she ran as fast **as** a cheetah.

Situation – time and place of a speech

Situational audience analysis – analyzing the audience based on the size of the audience, setting of the speech, attitudes toward the topic, attitudes toward the speaker, and occasion

Slippery slope – fallacy; one step will inadvertently lead to the next and so on

Small group – group of 3-20

Spatial pattern of arrangement – describing the physical proximity of the place or object

Speaker – person delivering a message

Speaker credibility – includes speaker's expertise, trustworthiness, similarity, and physical attractiveness

Special encyclopedia – contains more detailed information about a specific topic

Special occasion speech – includes speeches of introduction, presentation, acceptance, roasts and toasts, eulogies, and dinner speeches

Specific purpose – what the speaker wants to accomplish in the speech

Speech of introduction – introduces main speaker to audience

Speech of presentation – gives someone a gift, award, or recognition

Speech to gain immediate action – persuasive speech seeking agreement and inciting action

Speech for passive agreement – persuasive speech seeking agreement but needing no action

Sponsoring organization – when there is no author the organization is typically responsible for the content

Stage fright – the feeling of nervousness when going in front of people to perform or speak

Statistics – numerical data

Stereotyping- oversimplification of a person based on a few demographical attributes (e.g. all women are motherly, all men are "macho")

Strategic organization – putting a speech together to achieve a result

Supporting materials – material used to support a speech (examples, statistics, testimony)

Symposium – several people speak on different aspects of same topic

Syllogism – three part argument; major premise, minor premise, and conclusion

Synonym – two words that mean the same thing

Talking head – a person that is stationary during the entirety of the speech

Target audience – the broader audience that will most likely be influenced by the speech

Testimony – findings, eyewitness accounts, and opinions

Thesaurus – a book of synonyms

Topic – subject of a speech

Topical pattern of arrangement – all topics are of equal importance and can be stated in any order

Transition – word or phrase that allow speaker to move fluidly between points

Uniform Resource Locator (URL) – website address

Vague question – questions that don't give enough information

Values – peoples beliefs on what is good or bad (these characteristics are hardest to change)

Virtual library – combines Internet and library for research

Visualization – mentally imagining success

Vocal fillers – unnecessary filling of silences (with sounds like "ummm")

Yearbook – a reference book that is published annually (e.g. Farmer's Almanac)

PRACTICE TEST

If you can answer about half of the questions correctly you should be in good shape. To be safe, strive for a 75% on this examination.

1. Which of the following is NOT a way to improve listening?
    a. Take strong notes
    b. Avoid distractions
    c. Focus
    d. Research the topic being discussed
    e. Suspend judgment

2. Used to signal the ending of a thought, and controls impact.
    a. Volume
    b. Rate
    c. Pitch
    d. Pause
    e. Dialect

3. A dyadic communication is?
    a. A communication via mass media
    b. A communication between two people
    c. A communication that is not received
    d. A misunderstanding of the shared meaning of a message
    e. A conversation referring to an anecdote

4. Specialized language that should be avoided during a public speech is called _____.
    a. Jargon
    b. Cliché
    c. Generic "he"
    d. Hate language
    e. Clutter

5. A brief summary of an article NOT written by the author is a(n) _____.
    a. Review
    b. Criticism
    c. Opinion
    d. Abstract
    e. Introduction

6. What is the definition of the mean of a group of numbers?
    a. The middle number
    b. The most common number
    c. The average of the numbers
    d. The numbers displayed graphically
    e. The square root of the numbers

7. Words that identify where the speaker is in the speech are called _____.
    a. Transitions
    b. Connectives
    c. Signposts
    d. Introductions
    e. Conclusions

8. An appeal to moral character is called?
    a. Emotional
    b. Ethos
    c. Guilt
    d. Logos
    e. Hindsight

9. Part of speech that enables identification of ethnicity.
    a. Dialect
    b. Articulation
    c. Pitch
    d. Rate
    e. Volume

10. An appeal to logic is called?
    a. An ethical appeal
    b. Ethos
    c. Logos
    d. Argument
    e. Reason

11. If you are running short on time what should you do?
    a. Talk fast so you can get all of the information in
    b. Highlight the main points only
    c. Create a bond with the audience
    d. Stop and reschedule the speech
    e. Continue past the time limit

12. Controlling anxiety in order to help make the speech a success is _____.
    a. Positive nervousness
    b. Visualization
    c. Stage fright
    d. Focused nervousness
    e. Performance anxiety

13. Which of the following is NOT a way to improve listening?
    a. Don't judge
    b. Listen for main points
    c. Focus
    d. Take notes
    e. All of the above are ways to improve listening

14. Which of the following does NOT need to be considered before using evidence?
    a. Author background
    b. Publication credibility
    c. Data reliability
    d. Publication date
    e. All of the above are necessary

15. What is wrong with the following interview question: Who is the principal of the school?
    a. The question is leading.
    b. The question is hostile.
    c. The question is direct.
    d. The question isn't open.
    e. The question could have been answered without the interview.

16. What is NOT one of the obstacles to listening?
    a. Listening too hard
    b. Not concentrating
    c. Self-centered listening
    d. Jumping to conclusions
    e. All of the above are examples of obstacles

17. A speech to give thanks for public recognition is a(n) _____ speech.
    a. Acceptance
    b. Generous
    c. Recipient
    d. Thank You
    e. None of the above

Use the following for questions 18-22
    I. Topical pattern of arrangement
    II. Chronological pattern of arrangement
    III. Narrative pattern of arrangement
    IV. Circle pattern of arrangement
    V. Problem-solution pattern of arrangement

18. A speech that outlines the issues of Earth's limited natural resources; then discusses how we can alleviate some of the problem by recycling.
    a. I
    b. II
    c. III
    d. IV
    e. V

19. A public speaker who tells a story to the audience is using:
    a. I
    b. II
    c. III
    d. IV
    e. V

20. A speech arranged as follows:

- Overpopulation of animal shelters.
- Pets are adopted or purchased at Christmas.
- Family's tire of pets and animals are sent back to the pound by spring.
- Overpopulation of animal shelters.

    a. I
    b. II
    c. III
    d. IV
    e. V

21. The presentation of topics where one topic is relational/dependent on the next:
    a. I
    b. II
    c. III
    d. IV
    e. V

22. A speech where all topics are equally important and are not dependent on another point (they can be presented in any order):
    a. I
    b. II
    c. III
    d. IV
    e. V

23. Which Amendment grants the right to free speech?
    a. First Amendment
    b. Second Amendment
    c. Fourth Amendment
    d. Sixth Amendment
    e. Ninth Amendment

24. The crispness of distinct speech sounds.
    a. Pronunciation
    b. Articulation
    c. Volume
    d. Pitch
    e. Rate

25. She laughs like a hyena is an example of a ____.
    a. Personification
    b. Assonance
    c. Metaphor
    d. Simile
    e. None of the above

Use the following paragraph for questions 26-30

Mr. Brown is speaking about the Just Say No to drug ad campaign (A). He wants to influence the children's attitudes (B) about drugs. The final outcome is that he wants children to stay away from drugs (C). He is going to discuss the dangers of drugs for health and social activities (D). He believes that if he can scare the children (E) enough, they surely will not try drugs.

26. Which of the following is an example of an emotional appeal?
    a. Just Say No to drug ad campaign
    b. Influence the children's attitudes
    c. Children to stay away from drugs
    d. He is going to discuss the dangers of drugs on health and social activities
    e. Scare the children

27. Which of the following is the topic?
    a. Just Say No to drug ad campaign
    b. Influence the children's attitudes
    c. Children to stay away from drugs
    d. He is going to discuss the dangers of drugs for health and social activities
    e. Scare the children

28. What is the central idea of the speech?
    a. Just Say No to drug ad campaign
    b. Influence the children's attitudes
    c. Children to stay away from drugs
    d. He is going to discuss the dangers of drugs for health and social activities
    e. Scare the children

29. What is the specific purpose of the speech?
    a. Just Say No to drug ad campaign
    b. Influence the children's attitudes
    c. Children to stay away from drugs
    d. He is going to discuss the dangers of drugs for health and social activities
    e. Scare the children

30. What is the general purpose of the speech?
    a. Just Say No to drug ad campaign
    b. Influence the children's attitudes
    c. Children to stay away from drugs
    d. He is going to discuss the dangers of drugs for health and social activities
    e. Scare the children

Use the following for questions 31-35
   I.   Appreciative listening
   II. Not listening
   III. Empathetic listening
   IV. Comprehensive listening
   V.   Critical listening

31. Jane put her headphones on to listen to music.
    a. I
    b. II
    c. III
    d. IV
    e. V

32. Frank was listening to his teenager discuss why she wasn't home by curfew. He was trying to determine if she was telling the truth.
    a. I
    b. II
    c. III
    d. IV
    e. V

33. The toddler was talking to his mother while she was reading the paper. She responded automatically with "oh, my, is that so?"
    a. I
    b. II
    c. III
    d. IV
    e. V

34. Jack received a call from Mary. Mary was upset; she talked to him about her grandmother falling ill.
    a. I
    b. II
    c. III
    d. IV
    e. V

35. The teacher held a lecture on the Civil War. The students were listening and taking notes.
    a. I
    b. II
    c. III
    d. IV
    e. V

36. Delivering a speech with almost no preparation time is called a(n) _____ speech.
    a. Manuscript
    b. Memorized
    c. Impromptu
    d. Extemporaneous
    e. Special Occasion

Use the following for questions 37-41.

      I.   Parallelism
      II.   Repetition
      III.   Antithesis
      IV.   Alliteration
      V.   Simile

37. "Ask not what your country can do for you, but what you can do for your country," John F. Kennedy.
    a. I
    b. II
    c. III
    d. IV
    e. V

38. "Reading maketh a full man, conference a ready man, and writing an exact man," Francis Bacon.
    a. I
    b. II
    c. III
    d. IV
    e. V

39. "We will not tire, we will not falter and we will not fail'" George W. Bush.
    a. I
    b. II
    c. III
    d. IV
    e. V

40. "My love is like a red, red rose," Robert Burns.
    a. I
    b. II
    c. III
    d. IV
    e. V

41. ""Let us go forth to lead the land we love," John F. Kennedy.
    a. I
    b. II
    c. III
    d. IV
    e. V

Use the following for questions 42-46
   I.   Quotations
   II. Global plagiarism
   III. Paraphrasing
   IV. Patchwork plagiarism
   V.   Incremental plagiarism

42. Ideas taken from multiple sources:
    a. I
    b. II
    c. III
    d. IV
    e. V

43. Rewording someone else's ideas into your words:
    a. I
    b. II
    c. III
    d. IV
    e. V

44. Telling someone word for word what someone else said:
    a. I
    b. II
    c. III
    d. IV
    e. V

45. Passing someone else's idea off in its entirety as your own:
    a. I
    b. II
    c. III
    d. IV
    e. V

46. Failure to give credit to someone else in part of a speech:
    a. I
    b. II
    c. III
    d. IV
    e. V

47. George is listening to a candidate running for senate. He is trying to determine if he wants to vote for the candidate. What type of listening is George doing?
    a. Appreciative
    b. Empathetic
    c. Comprehensive
    d. Critical
    e. Ethical

48. Elise is speaking with Sarah on the telephone. The telephone is an example of the _____.
    a. Mode
    b. Method
    c. Channel
    d. Feedback
    e. Interference

49. Which of the following is a way to boost credibility?
    a. Explanation of why you are an expert
    b. Creating a bond with the audience
    c. Speaking like you mean it
    d. None of the above
    e. All of the above

Use the following for paragraph to answer questions 50 through 52:

Mary was introduced to an auditorium of children by the principal, Mrs. Winter. Mary's purpose was to discuss Earth Day. During the course of her speech the microphone cut in and out making her difficult to understand. The children began to get fidgety and put their hands behind their ears to hear Mary. However, one little boy, Jason decided he wouldn't try to hear and began singing "Happy Birthday" in the middle of her speech!

50. What is an example of feedback?
    a. Jason
    b. Children putting their hands behind their ears
    c. Microphone not working
    d. Mrs. Winter's introduction
    e. Earth day

51. What is the channel?
    a. Auditorium
    b. Microphone
    c. Mrs. Winter
    d. Children
    e. Both A and B

52. What was interference?
    a. Microphone cutting in and out
    b. Children putting their hands behind their ears
    c. Jason's song
    d. All of the above
    e. A and C

53. All women like to cook is an example of?
    a. Racism
    b. Stereotyping
    c. Simplification
    d. Fact
    e. Criticism

54. When the speaker began, a hush fell over the audience. Is an example of:
    a. Simile
    b. Metaphor
    c. Hyperbole
    d. Cliché
    e. Alliteration

55. What is wrong with this sentence?
When a soldier fights overseas, he understands his sacrifice.
    a. Too much clutter
    b. Global use of the word "he"
    c. Alliteration
    d. All of the above
    e. A and B

Use the following for questions 56-60

I. Fair use
II. Frame of reference
III. Personal inventory
IV. Clustering
V. Implied leader

56. Writing the first things that come to mind in nine areas. (For the purpose of finding a speech topic).
    a. I
    b. II
    c. III
    d. IV
    e. V

57. Law that makes it legal for teachers and students to use copyrighted material for the sake of education.
    a. I
    b. II
    c. III
    d. IV
    e. V

58. Person that is in charge based on seniority.
    a. I
    b. II
    c. III
    d. IV
    e. V

59. Writing down all hobbies and interests to try to find a speech topic.
    a. I
    b. II
    c. III
    d. IV
    e. V

60. A person's values and beliefs
    a. I
    b. II
    c. III
    d. IV
    e. V

61. "What goes around, comes around", "live and learn", "look before you leap" are all examples of:
    a. Jargon
    b. Simile
    c. Cliché
    d. Metaphor
    e. Alliteration

Use the following for questions 62-66
- I. Competence
- II. Initial credibility
- III. Character
- IV. Derived credibility
- V. Terminal credibility

62. Ms. O'hare provided a brief introduction for Mr. White. She did not speak of his expertise. This largely affected his _____?
    a. I
    b. II
    c. III
    d. IV
    e. V

63. During Mr. White's introduction in his speech he demonstrated his _____ by discussing his extensive experience in the subject.
    a. I
    b. II
    c. III
    d. IV
    e. V

64. As Mr. White went through his speech the audience believed that he was an expert on his topic. This is an example of _____.
    a. I
    b. II
    c. III
    d. IV
    e. V

65. The audience believed that Mr. White was trustworthy with good intentions. This is a reflection of his _____.
    a. I
    b. II
    c. III
    d. IV
    e. V

66. The audience left the speech believing that Mr. White was an expert on his subject.
    a. I
    b. II
    c. III
    d. IV
    e. V

67. Which type of example is one that hasn't happened, but MAY happen?
    a. Possibility example
    b. Hypothetical example
    c. Brief example
    d. Extended example
    e. Expert example

68. Sally was listening to her friend complain about a bad day at work. She is performing what type of listening?
    a. Appreciative
    b. Empathetic
    c. Comprehensive
    d. Critical
    e. Apathetic

69. Which of the following is NOT an example of a reference work?
    a. Encyclopedia
    b. Almanac
    c. Dictionary
    d. Quotation book
    e. Newspaper

Use the following for questions 70-74
- I. Red herring
- II. Ad hominem
- III. Bandwagon
- IV. Either/or
- V. Slippery slope

70. The fallacy that the first step in a process will subsequently lead to future steps.
    - a. I
    - b. II
    - c. III
    - d. IV
    - e. V

71. The following is an example of _____ fallacy: The president, who was never a member of the military, will advocate mandatory military service.
    - a. I
    - b. II
    - c. III
    - d. IV
    - e. V

72. The following is an example of _____ fallacy: The highly liberal, spend-happy candidate wants to spend all of our hard-earned tax dollars for her inconsequential plan.
    - a. I
    - b. II
    - c. III
    - d. IV
    - e. V

73. The following is an example of _____ fallacy: Since everyone is doing it, adoption from a foreign country is the best method.
    - a. I
    - b. II
    - c. III
    - d. IV
    - e. V

74. The following is an example of _____ fallacy: High school graduates can either go to college, or join the military.
    a. I
    b. II
    c. III
    d. IV
    e. V

75. What kind of reasoning is the following:

    All people need food.
    I am a person.
    I need food.

    a. Analogical
    b. Causal
    c. Principle
    d. Specifics
    e. Detail oriented

76. Which type of reasoning is the following:
    If you like gymnastics you'll be a great cheerleader.
    a. Analogical
    b. Causal
    c. Principle
    d. Specifics
    e. Detail oriented

77. So far we have determined that the cause for many family's economic circumstances have been caused by involuntary job loss. The pervious statement is an example of _____.
    a. Internal preview
    b. Signpost
    c. Transition
    d. Internal summary
    e. Conclusion

78. As a teacher the general purpose of public speaking is?
    a. Inform
    b. Appeal
    c. Persuade
    d. Entertain
    e. None of the above

79. If there is no author identified on a document/website try to determine the _____.
    a. Sponsoring organization
    b. Publisher
    c. Webmaster
    d. Email address
    e. Collaborator

80. The anxiety before giving a speech is called?
    a. Visualization
    b. Stage fright
    c. Adrenaline
    d. Endorphins
    e. None of the above

81. The belief that one culture is superior to another:
    a. Egocentrism
    b. Egotistic
    c. Ethnocentrism
    d. Elitist
    e. Egalitarian

82. The typical nonverbal message that listeners deliver to the speaker is _____.
    a. Feedback
    b. Prompts
    c. Note taking
    d. Cues
    e. Body language

83. The three main parts of a speech are called:
    a. Beginning, middle, end
    b. Beginning, body, summary
    c. Introduction, body, conclusion
    d. Introduction, body, summary
    e. Introduction, middle, conclusion

84. People's natural inclination to be concerned with themselves before others is:
    a. Egalitarian
    b. Egocentrism
    c. Egotistic
    d. Elitist
    e. Ethnocentrism

ANSWER KEY

1. D. Research the topic being discussed is not one of the ways to improve listening skills.
2. D. A pause signals the end of a thought and the impact of a point.
3. B. Dyadic communication is between two people.
4. A. Jargon is specialized language to a specific group of people.
5. D. An abstract is a summary of content not written by the author.
6. C. The mean is the average of a group of numbers.
7. C. Signposts identify where the speaker is in the speech.
8. B. Ethos is an appeal to moral character.
9. A. Dialect is the clearest indicator of ethnicity.
10. C. Logos is an appeal to logic.
11. B. If time is running short, be sure to highlight the main points of your speech.
12. A. Positive nervousness is focusing nervousness for a good speech outcome.

13. E. All of the above (listening for main points, focusing, taking notes, and withholding judgment) are ways to improve listening.

14. E. Author, publication date, publication credibility, and background should all be considered before using evidence.

15. E. Questions that can be answered without an interview should not be asked.

16. E. Listening too hard, not concentrating, self-centered listening and jumping to conclusions are all examples of obstacles to listening.

17. A. A speech to give thanks for public recognition is an acceptance speech.

18. E. This speech would be a problem (Earth's resources dwindling)/ solution (recycle) speech.

19. C. Telling a story is a narrative.

20. D. The circle arrangement starts at a topic (overpopulation of the pound) and comes back to the topic.

21. B. Chronological speech points are directly dependent on one another.

22. A. Topical speech points can stand-alone and are not dependent on other speech points.

23. A. The First Amendment grants the right to free speech.

24. B. Articulation is the distinct speech sound.

25. D. Simile is comparing two unlike things using the words "like" or "as".

26. E. Emotional appeal can use fear to try to achieve the objective.

27. A. Just Say No ad campaign is the topic of this speech.

28. D. The central idea discusses the main ideas.

29. C. The specific purpose is to stop kids from using drugs.

30. B. The general purpose is to persuade (influence attitudes of the children).

31. A. Appreciative listening is to enjoy.

32. E. Critical listening is to determine truthfulness.

33. B. Hearing and listening is not the same thing.

34. C. Empathetic listening is to comfort.

35. D. Comprehensive listening is to understand.

36. C. An impromptu speech is a speech orated with little to no preparation time.

37. C. Kennedy used the juxtaposition of words (antithesis) to tell people what they should do.

38. A. Bacon uses parallelism to describe his point.

39. B. Bush uses repetition for impact.

40. E. Burns uses simile to compare his love to a red rose.

41. D. Kennedy uses alliteration with the consonant "L".

42. D. Patchwork plagiarism is taking many ideas from others and passing them off as your own.

43. C. Paraphrasing is rewording someone else's ideas into your own words.

44. A. Quotes is someone else's words altogether (not passed off as your own).

45. B. Global plagiarism is taking someone else's entire idea and passing it off as your own.

46. E. Incremental plagiarism is failing to give credit to someone for their idea in parts of a speech.

47. D. George is critically listening to the candidate to determine the validity of their stance.

48. C. The telephone is the channel for a phone conversation.

49. E. Explaining why you should be considered an expert, speaking with conviction, and creating a bond with the audience are all ways to boost credibility.

50. B. The children putting their hands behind their ears to try to hear is an example of feedback.

51. B. The microphone is the channel.

52. E. The microphone and Jason's song both interfered with Mary's message.

53. B. To say that all women like to cook is an example of stereotyping based on demographics.

54. B. A hush fell over the audience is a metaphor.

55. B. The global "he" is the problem with the statement.

56. D. Clustering is writing the first things that come to mind in nine columns to find a speech topic.

57. A. Fair use is the ability for teachers and students to use copyrighted material for educational purposes.

58. E. The implied leader is the one that emerges from seniority.

59. C. Personal inventory is the writing of one's interests and hobbies to try to find a speech topic.

60. B. The frame of reference is a person's values and beliefs.

61. C. Clichés are overused expressions.

62. B. Initial credibility is how the audience feels about the speaker before the speaker begins.

63. A. Competence is the perceived expertise of the speaker.

64. D. Derived credibility is the credibility the audience perceives during the speech.
65. C. Character is the perceived trustworthiness of the speaker.
66. E. Terminal credibility is how the audience feels about the speaker after the conclusion.
67. B. A hypothetical example is one that discusses possibilities.
68. B. Listening as a counselor/friend is empathetic listening.
69. E. A newspaper is not a reference work.
70. E. The slippery slope fallacy assumes that the first step taken will inevitably lead to subsequent steps.
71. A. The red herring fallacy focuses on something to divert the attention from the true topic (the president's inexperience in the military).
72. B. The ad hominem fallacy attacks the person instead of the issue.
73. C. The bandwagon fallacy assumes that popularity of a view means it is correct.
74. D. The either/or fallacy assumes there are only two options when others exist.

75. C. Principle reasoning uses principles to reason to a conclusion.

76. A. Analogical reasoning compares two seemingly alike things to reach a conclusion.

77. A. An internal summary is when the points are summarized within the speech.

78. A. Teachers typically speak to inform.

79. A. If no author can be identified on a document try to determine the sponsoring organization.

80. B. Stage fright is the anxiety over the idea of giving a speech.

81. C. Ethnocentrism is the idea that one culture is superior to another.

82. A. Feedback is usually a nonverbal form of communication that the audience gives to the speaker.

83. C. Introduction, body, and conclusion are the three main parts of a speech.

84. B. Egocentrism is when people are more concerned with themselves before others.

INDEX

alliteration, 32, 59, 83, 87, 88
antithesis, 32, 60, 83
appeals
   emotional, 24
articulation, 33, 48, 60, 76, 79, 97
audience analysis, 10, 46, 49
audience centeredness, 12
brainstorm, 14
central idea, 17, 19, 43, 81, 97
channel, 8, 61, 85
clustering, 14, 87, 99
Consideration
   ethical, historical, social, 8, 46, 47
Considerations
   ethical, historical, social, 8
credibility, 21, 22, 62
delivery
   methods of, 34
fallacies, 23
   ad hominem, 23
   bandwagon, 24
   either or, 23
   red herring, 23, 71, 91
   slippery slope, 24
feedback, 8, 37, 65, 85, 93, 101
free speech issues, 9
general purpose, 16, 17, 42, 81, 93, 97
identification, 12, 76
imagery, 24, 31
interference, 8, 66, 85
listener, 8, 67
listening, 36
   types of, 37
message, 8, 68
organizational strategy
   causal, 20
   chronological, 20, 61, 78, 96
   problem solution, 20
   spatial, 20, 72
   topical, 20
parallelism, 32, 69, 83
paraphrase, 9, 69
plagiarism, 9, 65, 66, 69, 84, 98
plaigiarism
   global, 9, 65, 84, 87, 98
   incremental, 9, 66, 84, 98
   patchwork, 9, 69, 84, 98
public speaking, 6, 16
questions
   fixed-alternative, 11
   open-ended, 11
   scale, 11, 68
quotations, 9
Quotations, 84
reasoning, 21, 23, 39, 47, 59, 61, 64, 92, 101
   analogical, 23
   casual, 23
   principle, 23
   specifics, 23
repetition, 32, 71, 83
situation, 8, 72
situational audience analysis, 10, 12
speaker, 8, 11, 72
speaking apprehension, 35
specific purpose, 12, 16, 17, 19, 42, 81, 97
speeches
   body, 18
   conclusion, 19
   introduction, 18
   structure of, 18

stereotyping, 10, 99
supporting materials, 21
   evidence, 21
topics of speeches, 14
value, 16, 70
visual aids, 26

voice, 33
   pause, 33, 69, 75
   pitch, 33
   pronunciation, 33
   volume, 27, 33, 75, 76, 80

Made in the USA
San Bernardino, CA
01 February 2013